The Call of Kumayl

Translated by

Taher Al-Shemaly

Published by Left of Brain Books

Copyright © 2023 Left of Brain Books

ISBN 978-1-397-66526-3

First Edition

All rights reserved. No part of this publication may be reproduced, distributed, or transmitted in any form or by any means, including photocopying, recording, or other electronic or mechanical methods, without the prior written permission of the publisher, except in the case of brief quotations permitted by copyright law. Left of Brain Books is a division of Left Of Brain Onboarding Pty Ltd.

PUBLISHER'S PREFACE

About the Book

A Shiite prayer.

CONTENTS

PUBLISHER'S PREFACE
   TRANSLATOR'S WORD 1
   ENGLISH 3
   ARABIC 15

TRANSLATOR'S WORD

THIS is what is called the "Call of Kumayl." The word "Call" needs a little explanation here. In fact the form of this text is the same as a prayer, but since the verb "to pray" has different aspects in different cultures I decided here to use the verb "to call" for this piece. While in christian literature the verb "to pray" means mainly asking for help from God, the very same verb has another meaning in islamic literature. The verb "to pray" in Islam has the meaning of doing the worshipping which is done by any muslim everyday, or mainly the 5 main prayers of the day, but to ask God for help or a text that is meant to be in a form of a soliloquy between oneself and God, is much closer to the word "Call" because such text is called in Arabic "Do`â'" which stems from the verb "to call" in Arabic.

The Call you are going to pass by next is a familiar text for (almost) any shiite muslim who keeps up with his religious duties. The main body of the call is between the asterisks.

This is a rough translation with as simple as possible English. Such texts would be better to be translated in a form of literature English, but the idea here is to pass some cultural exchange to the other side of the world. The beauty of such text would be better exmained by people who can read Arabic, since it rhymes more and the wide range of words used in Arabic add up more to the sense of faith inside the reader, if he/she knows what is read.

Some markers:
(PUH): Peace Upon Him

(...): further translation and/or explanation
[...]: my own note

Taher Al-Shemaly (TJ)
Kuwait

ENGLISH

The call (or pray) of Kumayl is in fact the call of Al-Khidhr (PUH), but it
was called like that because the prince of the believers (PUH) taught this
call to Kumayl bin Ziyâd Al-Nakh`ee and for this it was named after him.
This call is considered one of the most famous calls and considered one of
the best, and it is preferred to read this call in the night of the middle of
the month of Sha`bân [8th month] and in every Friday's night [That is Thursday night in
the solar calendars because in lunar calendars the day begins first by
night]. Al-Sayid bin Tâwoos told in the book of "Al-Iqabâl" within a long
speech [as reported from the prince of believers (PUH)]: if you memorized this call then read it every Friday's night, or once a month, or once a year, or once in a life time, thus you shall be protected and victorious and mercy shall be always there for you, O Kumayl I
guarantee for you as long you are with us (The Household of Mohammed) so we
shall answer your desires generously. Then he said: write (O Kumayl) -then
this he wrote- :

In the name of Allah, the Beneficent, the Merciful

O Lord I ask You by Your mercy that befell on everything
and by Your power by which You mastered everything
and everything became under it
and everything became enslaved to it
and by Your might by which You defeated everything
and by Your glory that nothing stands before it
and by Your greatness that filled everything
and by Your majesty that came over everything
and by Your face that will remain after the vanishing of everything
and by Your Names that filled the corners of everything
and by Your knowledge that surrounded everything
and by the light of Your face that enlighted everything
Yâ Noor (O Light) Yâ Quddoos (O Most Holy) O The First of all and The Last
of all
O Lord forgive me the sins that break up the safety
O Lord forgive me the sins that reveal the resentments
O Lord forgive me the sins that change the gifts (of You)
O Lord forgive me the sins that imprison the call
O Lord forgive me the sins that reveal the adversities
O Lord forgive me every sin I sinned, and every mistake I have mistaken
O Lord I approach You by mentioning Your Name and get closer to You by You
and I shall ask You to get me closer to You and to spread Your thanks over
me and inspire me to mention Your Name
O Lord I ask You as an obeying, enslaved and humble man, to forgive me and
have mercy upon me and make me satisfied with Your division (destiny) and in
all situations to be humble
O Lord I ask You as he whom adversities befell on him severely, and at

troubles revealed his needs by Your doors, and as he who his desires were
before You
O Lord great is Your majesty
and high is Your place
and hidden is Your cunning
and obvious is Your reality
and victorious is Your might
and went on Your ability
and there is no escape from Your own government
O Lord I do not find for my sins a forgiver
and no one for my ugliness to be covering
and nothing of my bad deeds to be exchanged with good except of You
no other God but You, Be glorified and thanked. I wronged myself and I dared
by my ingnorance and took refuge by Your old mention of me and Your grace
over me
O Lord how many ugly things You have hidden
and how many a great adversity You have relieved
and how many a misstep You have prevented
and how many a mishap You have pushed away
and how many a praise of me that I'm not worthy for You have spreaded
O Lord great is my adversity
and gratified is my bad situation
and my (good) deeds have been shortened
and my chains brought me down
and my far hopes kept me away from my own benefit
and life tricked me by its arrogance
and my soul by its crime and my procrastination
O my Lord then shall I ask You by Your majesty that my call shall not be blocked by my

bad deeds
and do not dishonor me with what You have known about my secrets
and do not hurry Your punishment for me for what I did in my privacy of the
bad deeds, and my missing and my ignorance, and my abundant lust and
incaution
O Lord and be for me by Your majesty in all situations a merciful and for me in all the matters a passionate
O Lord and my God whoever I have to ask to relieve my adversity and to look
at my matter except of You?
O Lord and my Master, You have judged me for following the lust of my soul
and was not careful how my enemy (devil) ornamented (things for me), and he tricked me with
what I have lust for and with what makes him happy for this judgement. Thus
I passed over some of Your limitations and I went against some of Your
commandments, and Your grace for all of that is over me and I have no excuse
before Your judgement and what befell me of Your commands and adversities
and here I come O my Lord after my negligence and my extravagance for
myself, apologizing, regretting, broken, lonely, asking for mercy, repenting, recognizing, obeying, admitting, can't find any escape of what I
did and no refuge to take for my matters except of You accepting my apology,
and getting me into Your wide mercy
O Lord accept my apology and have mercy upon my severe adversity and release

me from my tight lashing
O Lord have mercy upon the weakness of my body and the softness of my skin
and the brittleness of my bones
O You who started my creation and my mention and my education and took care
of me and feeded me, make me for the beginning of Your generosity and the
previous of Your care towards me
O my Lord and my Master and My God, shall You torture me with Your hell
after unifying You? and after my heart having the knowledge about You and my
tongue mentioned Your Name and after what my conscience believed about Your
love, and after the truthful confession from me for Your deity?
How impossible! You are more generous than making who You have grown up go
astray
or send him far he who You have made close
or stray who You have nestled
or give him to the adversities he who You have protected and had mercy upon
and I wish my poem [expression of wishing in Arabic] O my Lord and my God
and my Master
shall You order the fire to be on faces that fell down for Your greatness
prostrating?
and on tongues that mentioned Your unity truthfully?
and praising You with thanks
and on hearts admitted Your deity faithfully
and on consciences gained the knowledge until they became humble before You

and on feelings that went on the lands to worship You obeying (You) and
started to repent before You
This is not the thought about You and not what we were told about Your
generosity O Generous One, O Lord
and You know my weakness before few of the adversities in this life and its
punishments and what happens of troubles to those living in it, but that is
an adversity that will not last long and easy to handle with a short period
of time, then how shall I bear the adversities of the afterlife and its
great mishaps, and it is an adversity that will last long and placed for
eternity and it is never lowered down for those in it because it does not
become unless for Your anger and Your revenge, and this is something that
heavens and earth cannot bear
O my Lord then how I shall be and I am Your weak slave, the humble, the
poor, the miserable
O my Lord and my God and my Master, what to You shall I complain about, and
what to You shall I cry out loud about?
for the painful torture and its hardness?
or for the long lasting of adversity and its longevity?
and if You made me for the punishments with Your enemies and gathered me
with the people of Your adversities and separated me from Your beloved and
viceroys, then suppose my Master and my Lord and my God I had patient with

Your torture then how shall I be patient for being away from You?

and suppose I stood the heat of Your hell, then how shall I be patient for

not looking at Your generosity?

or how shall I be in hell and I have hope in Your forgiveness?

then by Your own majesty O my Master and my Lord, I swear truthfully that if

You left me speaking then I shall scream to You among its people (hell) the

scream of those with hopes, and I shall shout as those shouting for help,

and I shall cry for You as the cry of those who lost dear ones, and I shall

call You and say where have You been O patron of believers?

O goal of the hopes of the wisemen

O Helper of those asking for help

O who is beloved to the hearts of the believers

O God of the worlds

shall You, be glorified Your Name, O my God and by Your grace, hear the

sound of a muslim slave that was imprisoned in it for going against You? and

tasted its torture by his sins? and was kept between its jaws for his crime

and mistake? and he is shouting to You as one with hope for Your mercy, and

call You with the tongue of the people who unified You, and beg You by Your

own deity

O my Lord then how shall he remain in the torture and he is wishing for the

past of Your mercy?

or how shall the hell hurt him and he hopes for Your generosity to release
him from it?
or how shall he would be burned by its fires and You hear him and see his
place?
or how shall he be incuded in its exhalations and You know how weak he is?
or how shall he be kept among its claws and You know how truthful he is?
or how shall he be rebuked by its keepers (angels of punishment) and he is
calling You "O my Lord!" ?
or how shall he be willing for Your generosity and You leave him in it?
How impossible! This is not the thought about You, and that is not what is
known of Your generosity, and it is not like how You treat the unifiers by
Your generosity and help
and certainly I am sure if it is not for what You promised of torture for
those who disbelieve in You, and Your judgement for those who go against You
to be eternal (in it), then surely You would make it be coolness and peace
and no one shall be living or dwelling there
but You, glorified Your Names, swore that You will fill it with
disbelievers, from the djinn and the human as well, and to make eternal in
it those who go against You
and You, gratified be Your praising, said in the beginning, and gave much of
Your favors by Your generosity

Is he who is a believer like unto him who is an evil-liver? They are not
alike
O my God and my Lord, then I shall ask You by the might that You have fixed,
and by the matter that You have destined and ruled, and defeated by it
whoever You have made it for, to forgive me in this night and this hour
every crime I have commited and every sin I have sinnned and every ugliness
I have made in secret, and every ignorance I have commited either announced
or been a secret, made it hidden or made it apparent, and every sin that You
have ordered the dignified writers (writing angels recording the deeds of a
man) to note down, those who You have made to save everything I do and made
them witnesses with my organs
and You have been the Watcher over me from their behind, and the Witness for
whatever was hidden from them and by Your mercy You have made it hidden
and (shall I ask) to make my luck abundant in every good You have revealed,
or a favor You have given, or a virtue that You have spreaded, or an income
that You have made easy, or a mistake that You have covered
O God, O God, O God, O my God and my Master and my Lord and the Owner of my
slavery, O You who has my matter in His hands, O You who know my adversity

and my humbleness, O You who best knows my poverty and my need

O God, O God, O God, I ask You by Your right and by Your glory, and by the

greatest of Your characters and Names, to make my times of the night and da

full of Your mention, and contiunous under Your service, and my deeds are

accepted by You, so that all my deeds and works be in one path, and my

situation in serving You would be eternal

O my Lord who helps me, O You who I complained to about my matters

O God, O God, O God, make my body strong enough to serve You

and tighten my soul on the strength, and give me the seriousness to fear

You, and the eternity to be under Your service, so that I shall be running

to You in the fields of the competents and hurry to You among those in the

beginning

and long for Your closeness among those craving (to You), and be close to

You like those faithful to You, and be afraid of You like those who know You

the best, and be gathered in Your closeness with the believers

O Lord and those whoever wanted to hurt me then hurt them, and whoever

wanted to trick me then trick them, and make me one of those of the best

favors from You, and the closest in place to You, and the most special in

proximity to You, because this is not to be begotten unless by Your favor,

and have grace on me by Your generosity, and have passion on me by Your own
glory and save me by Your own mercy
and make my tongue busy with Your mention
and my heart with Your love tightened
and have grace on me by the goodness of Your answer and relieve me from my
own missteps and forgive my mistake
and if You assigned to Your slaves to worship You and ordered them to call
for You and You have guaranteed the answer for them, so to You O God I turn
my face, and to You O God I expanded my hand
so by Your own might answer my call, and make me reach my own goal and do
not stop my hopes in Your own grace
and avoid me the evils of the djinn and the people from my enemies
O You who has satisfaction rapidly, forgive for he who has nothing but to
call You, because You are willing to do anything You want
O You who His Name is a cure, and His mention is a remedy, and obeying Him
is wealth
have mercy upon he who has nothing but hope, and his weapon is to cry
O You who has many favors
O You who pushes away the evils
O You who is the light of the lonely in the darkness
O You who knows best and never taught
have peace upon Mohammed and the Household of Mohammed
and do to me what is best by You

and may Allah have peace upon His prophet and the faithful viceroys of his
descendants, and may (He) greets them greatly.

ARABIC

اَللّـهُمَّ إِنِّي أَسْأَلُكَ بِرَحْمَتِكَ الَّتِي وَسِعَتْ كُلَّ شَيْءٍ ، وَ بِقُوَّتِكَ الَّتِي قَهَرْتَ بِهَا كُلَّ شَيْءٍ ، وَ خَضَعَ لَهَا كُلُّ شَيْءٍ ، وَ ذَلَّ لَهَا كُلُّ شَيْءٍ ، وَ بِجَبَرُوتِكَ الَّتِي غَلَبْتَ بِهَا كُلَّ شَيْءٍ ، وَ بِعِزَّتِكَ الَّتِي لا يَقُومُ لَهَا شَيْءٌ ، وَ بِعَظَمَتِكَ الَّتِي مَلأَتْ كُلَّ شَيْءٍ ، وَ بِسُلْطانِكَ الَّذِي عَلا كُلَّ شَيْءٍ ، وَ بِوَجْهِكَ الْباقِي بَعْدَ فَناءِ كُلِّ شَيْءٍ ، وَ بِأَسْمائِكَ الَّتِي مَلأَتْ أَرْكانَ كُلِّ شَيْءٍ ، وَ بِعِلْمِكَ الَّذِي أَحاطَ بِكُلِّ شَيْءٍ ، وَ بِنُورِ وَجْهِكَ الَّذِي أَضاءَ لَهُ كُلُّ شَيْءٍ ، يا نُورُ يا قُدُّوسُ ، يا أَوَّلَ الْأَوَّلِينَ وَ يا آخِرَ الْآخِرِينَ .
اَللّـهُمَّ اغْفِرْ لِي الذُّنُوبَ الَّتِي تَهْتِكُ الْعِصَمَ ، اَللّـهُمَّ اغْفِرْ لِي الذُّنُوبَ الَّتِي تُنْزِلُ النِّقَمَ ، اَللّـهُمَّ اغْفِرْ لِي الذُّنُوبَ الَّتِي تُغَيِّرُ النِّعَمَ ، اَللّـهُمَّ اغْفِرْ لِي الذُّنُوبَ الَّتِي تَحْبِسُ الدُّعاءَ ، اَللّـهُمَّ اغْفِرْ لِي كُلَّ ذَنْبٍ أَذْنَبْتُهُ ، وَ كُلَّ خَطِيئَةٍ أَخْطَأْتُها .
اَللّـهُمَّ إِنِّي أَتَقَرَّبُ إِلَيْكَ بِذِكْرِكَ ، وَ أَسْتَشْفِعُ بِكَ إِلى نَفْسِكَ ، وَ أَسْأَلُكَ بِجُودِكَ أَنْ تُدْنِيَنِي مِنْ قُرْبِكَ ، وَ أَنْ تُوزِعَنِي شُكْرَكَ ، وَ أَنْ تُلْهِمَنِي ذِكْرَكَ ، اَللّـهُمَّ إِنِّي أَسْأَلُكَ سُؤالَ خاضِعٍ مُتَذَلِّلٍ خاشِعٍ أَنْ تُسامِحَنِي وَ تَرْحَمَنِي وَ تَجْعَلَنِي بِقِسْمِكَ راضِياً قانِعاً ، وَ فِي جَمِيعِ الْأَحْوالِ مُتَواضِعاً .
اَللّـهُمَّ وَ أَسْأَلُكَ سُؤالَ مَنِ اشْتَدَّتْ فاقَتُهُ ، وَ أَنْزَلَ بِكَ عِنْدَ الشَّدائِدِ حاجَتَهُ ، وَ عَظُمَ فِيما عِنْدَكَ رَغْبَتُهُ .
اَللّـهُمَّ عَظُمَ سُلْطانُكَ ، وَ عَلا مَكانُكَ ، وَ خَفِيَ مَكْرُكَ ، وَ ظَهَرَ أَمْرُكَ ، وَ غَلَبَ قَهْرُكَ ، وَ جَرَتْ قُدْرَتُكَ ، وَ لا يُمْكِنُ الْفِرارُ مِنْ حُكُومَتِكَ .
اَللّـهُمَّ لا أَجِدُ لِذُنُوبِي غافِراً ، وَ لا لِقَبائِحِي ساتِراً ، وَ لا لِشَيْءٍ مِنْ عَمَلِيَ الْقَبِيحِ بِالْحَسَنِ مُبَدِّلاً ، غَيْرَكَ لا إِلـهَ إِلاَّ أَنْتَ ، سُبْحانَكَ وَ بِحَمْدِكَ ، ظَلَمْتُ نَفْسِي ، وَ تَجَرَّأْتُ بِجَهْلِي ، وَ سَكَنْتُ إِلى قَدِيمِ ذِكْرِكَ لِي وَ مَنِّكَ عَلَيَّ .
اَللّـهُمَّ مَوْلايَ كَمْ مِنْ قَبِيحٍ سَتَرْتَهُ ، وَ كَمْ مِنْ فادِحٍ مِنَ الْبَلاءِ أَقَلْتَهُ ، وَ كَمْ مِنْ عِثارٍ وَقَيْتَهُ ، وَ كَمْ مِنْ مَكْرُوهٍ دَفَعْتَهُ ، وَ كَمْ مِنْ ثَناءٍ جَمِيلٍ لَسْتُ أَهْلاً لَهُ نَشَرْتَهُ .
اَللّـهُمَّ عَظُمَ بَلائِي ، وَ أَفْرَطَ بِي سُوءُ حالِي ، وَ قَصَّرَتْ بِي أَعْمالِي ، وَ قَعَدَتْ بِي أَغْلالِي ، وَ حَبَسَنِي عَنْ نَفْعِي بُعْدُ أَمَلِي ، وَ خَدَعَتْنِي

فَأَسْأَلُكَ سَيِّدي يا مِطالي وَ ، يجنايتِها نَفْسي وَ ، يغُرُورِها الدُّنيا تَفْضَحْني لا وَ ، فِعالي وَ عَمَلي سُوءَ دُعائي عَنْكَ يَحْجُبُ لا أنْ يعِزَّتِكَ ما عَلى بِالعُقوبَةِ تَعاجِلْني لا وَ ، سِرِّي مِنْ عَلَيْهِ اطَّلَعْتَ ما يَخْفى وَ تَفْريطي دَوامَ وَ ، إساءَتي وَ فِعْلي سُوءَ مِنْ خَلَواتي في عِمِلتَهُ كُلِّ في لي يعِزَّتِكَ اللَّهُمَّ كُنْ وَ ، غَفْلَتي وَ شَهَواتي كَثْرَةِ وَ ، جَهالَتي . عَطُوفاً الأمُورِ جَميعِ في عَلَيَّ وَ ، رَؤوفاً الأحْوالِ
، أمْري في النَّظَرَ وَ ، ضُرّي كَشْفَ أسْأَلُكَ غَيْرُكَ لي مَنْ رَبِّي وَ إلـهي لَمْ رَ وَ ، نَفْسي هَوى فيهِ إتَبَعْتُ حُكْماً عَلَيَّ أجْرَيْتَ مَوْلايَ وَ إلهِي ذلِكَ عَلى أسْعَدَهُ وَ أهْوى ما قَفَرْني ، عَدُوّي تَزْيينٍ مِنْ فيهِ أحْتَرِسَ خالَفْتُ وَ ، حُدُودِكَ بَعْضَ ذلِكَ مِنْ عَلَيَّ جَرى بِما فَتَجاوَزْتَ ، القَضاءُ فيما لي حُجَّةَ لا وَ ، ذلِكَ جَميعِ في عَلَيَّ الحَمْدُ فَلَكَ ، أوامِرِكَ بَعْضَ . بَلاؤُكَ وَ حُكْمُكَ الزَّمَني وَ ، قَضاؤُكَ فيهِ عَلَيَّ جَرى
مُعْتَذِراً نَفْسي عَلى إسْرافي وَ تَقْصيري بَعْدَ إلـهي يا آتَيْتُكَ قَدْ وَ أجِدُ لا ، مُعْتَرِفاً مُذْعِناً مُقِرّاً مُنيباً مُسْتَغْفِراً مُسْتَقيلاً مُنْكَسِراً نادِماً قَبُولِكَ غَيْرَ ، أمْري في إلَيْهِ أتَوَجَّهُ مَفْزَعاً لا وَ ، مِنّي كانَ مِمّا مَفَرّاً . رَحْمَتِكَ سَعَةً في إيّايَ إدْخالِكَ وَ ، عُذْري
. وَثاقي شَدَّ مِنْ فُكَّني وَ ، ضُرِّ شِيدَّةَ ارْحَمْ وَ ، عُذْري فَاقْبَل اللَّهُمَّ بَدْأ مَنْ يا ، عَظْمي دِقَّةَ وَ ، جِلْدي رِقَّةَ وَ ، بَدَني ضَعْفَ ارْحَمْ رَبِّ يا وَ ، كَرَمِكَ لِابْتِداءِ هَبْني تَغْذِيَتي وَ يَرِّي وَ تَرْبِيَتي وَ ذِكْري وَ خَلْقي . بي بِرِّكَ سالِفِ
ما بَعْدَ وَ ، تَوْحيدِكَ بَعْدَ يَنارِكَ مُعَذِّبي أتْراكَ ، رَبِّي وَ سَيِّدي وَ إلـهي يا وَ ، ذِكْرِكَ مِنْ لِساني يهِ لَهِجَ وَ ، مَعْرِفتِكَ مِنْ قَلْبي عَلَيْهِ انْطَوى خاضِعاً دُعائي وَ اعْتِرافي صِدْقَ بَعْدَ وَ ، حُبَّكَ مِنْ ضَميري اعْتَقَدَهُ أدْنِيَتَهُ مِنْ تَبْعَدَ أوْ ، رِبَّيْتَهُ مَنْ تُضِيعَ أنْ مِنْ أكْرَمُ أنْتَ هَيْهاتَ ، لِرُبوبِيَّتِكَ لَيَّتَ وَ ، رَحْمَتَهُ وَ كَفَيْتَهُ مِنَ البَلاءِ إلَى تُسَلِّمَ أوْ ، آوَيْتَهُ مَنْ تُشَرِّدَ أوْ ، خَرَّتْ وُجوهِ عَلى النّارِ أتُسَلِّطُ ، مَوْلايَ وَ إلـهي وَ سَيِّدي يا شِعْرِي يَشْكُرَكَ وَ ، صادِقَةٍ يَتَوْحيدِكَ نَطَقَتْ الْسُنُ عَلَيَّ وَ ، ساجِدَةٌ لِعَظَمَتِكَ حَوَتْ ضَمائِرَ عَلَيَّ وَ ، مُحَقِّقَةٌ يَإلهَيَّتِكَ اعْتَرَفَتْ قُلُوبٍ عَلَيَّ وَ ، مادِحَةً أوْطانٍ إلى سَعَتْ جَوارِحَ عَلَيَّ وَ ، خاشِعَةٍ صارَتْ حَتّى يَكَ الْعِلْمِ مِنْ لا وَ ، يِكَ الظَّنُّ هَكَذا ما ، مُذْعِنَةً يَاسْتِغْفارِكَ آشارَتْ وَ ، طائِعَةً تَعَبُّدِكَ . عَنْكَ يِفَضْلِكَ أُخَيرْنا
، عُقُوباتِها وَ الدُّنيا بَلاءِ مِنْ قَليل عَنْ ضَعْفي تَعْلَمُ أنْتَ وَ رَبِّ يا كَريمُ يا مَكْرُوهٍ وَ بَلاءٍ ذلِكَ أنَّ عَلى ، أهْلِها عَلى المَكارِهِ مِنْ فيها يَجْري ما وَ ، الآخِرَةِ لِبَلاءِ احْتِمالي فَكَيْفَ ، مُدَّتُ قَصير ، بَقاؤُهُ يَسيرٌ ، مَكَثَهُ قَليلٌ وَ ، مَقامَهُ يَدومُ وَ ، مُدَّتُ تَطُولُ بَلاءٌ هُوَ وَ ، فيها المَكارِهِ وقُوعُ جَليلٌ وَ

، سَخَطِكَ وَ انْتِقَامِكَ وَ غَضَبِكَ عَنْ إِلَّا يَكُونُ لَا لِأَنَّهُ ، أَهْلِهِ عَنْ يُخَفَّفُ لَا أَنَا وَلِي فَكَيْفَ سَيِّدِي يَا ، الْأَرْضِ وَ السَّمَاوَاتِ لَهُ تَقُومُ لَا مَا هَذَا وَ . الْمُسْتَكِينُ الْمِسْكِينُ الْحَقِيرُ الذَّلِيلُ الضَّعِيفُ عَبْدُكَ
مِنْهَا لِمَا وَ ، أَشْكُو إِلَيْكَ الْأُمُورَ لِأَيِّ مَوْلَايَ وَ سَيِّدِي وَ رَبِّي وَ إِلَهِي يَا قَلِئِن ، مُدَّتِهِ وَ الْبَلَاءِ لِطُولِ أَمْ ، شِدَّتِهِ وَ الْعَذَابِ لَأَلِيمِ ، أَبْكِي وَ أَضِجُّ وَ ، بَلَائِكَ أَهْلِ بَيْنَ وَ بَيْنِي جَمَعْتَ وَ ، أَعْدَائِكَ مَعَ لِلْعُقُوبَاتِ صَيَّرْتَنِي وَ سَيِّدِي وَ إِلَهِي يَا فَهَبْنِي ، أَوْلِيَائِكَ وَ أَحِبَّائِكَ بَيْنَ وَ بَيْنِي فَرَّقْتَ هَبْنِي وَ ، فِرَاقِكَ عَلَى أَصْبِرُ فَكَيْفَ ، عَذَابِكَ عَلَى صَبَرْتُ رَبِّي وَ مَوْلَايَ كَيْفَ أَمْ ، كَرَامَتِكَ إِلَى النَّظَرِ عَنْ أَصْبِرُ فَكَيْفَ ، نَارِكَ حَرِّ عَلَى صَبَرْتُ أُقْسِمُ مَوْلَايَ وَ سَيِّدِي يَا فَعِزَّتِكَ ، عَفْوُكَ رَجَائِي وَ النَّارُ فِي أَسْكُنُ وَ ، الْآمِلِينَ ضَجِيجُ أَهْلِهَا بَيْنَ إِلَيْكَ لَأَضِجَّنَّ نَاطِقاً تَرَكْتَنِي لَئِنْ صَادِقاً وَ ، الْفَاقِدِينَ بُكَاءَ عَلَيْكَ لَأَبْكِيَنَّ وَ ، الْمُسْتَصْرِخِينَ صُرَاخَ إِلَيْكَ لَأَصْرُخَنَّ غِيَاثَ يَا ، الْعَارِفِينَ آمَالَ غَايَةَ يَا ، الْمُؤْمِنِينَ وَلِيَّ يَا كُنْتَ أَيْنَ لَأُنَادِيَنَّكَ . الْعَالَمِينَ إِلَهَ يَا وَ ، الصَّادِقِينَ قُلُوبِ حَبِيبَ يَا ، الْمُسْتَغِيثِينَ
مُسْلِمٍ عَبْدٍ صَوْتُ فِيهَا تَسْمَعُ يَحْمَدِكَ وَ إِلَهِي يَا سُبْحَانَكَ أَقْتَرَاكَ بَيْنَ حَبْسٍ وَ ، يَمْعَصِيَتِهِ عَذَابَهَا طَعْمَ ذَاقَ وَ ، يَمْخَالَفَتِهِ فِيهَا سُجِنَ وَ ، لِرَحْمَتِكَ مُؤَمِّلٌ ضَجِيجٌ إِلَيْكَ يَضِجُّ هُوَ وَ ، جَرِيرَتِهِ وَ يَجْرِمِهِ أَطْبَاقُهَا مَوْلَايَ يَا ، بِرُبُوبِيَّتِكَ إِلَيْكَ يَتَوَسَّلُ وَ ، تَوْحِيدِكَ أَهْلِ بِلِسَانٍ يُنَادِيكَ كَيْفَ أَمْ ، حِلْمِكَ مِنْ سَلَفَ مَا يَرْجُو هُوَ وَ الْعَذَابِ فِي يَبْقَى فَكَيْفَ أَنْتَ وَ لَهِيبُهَا يَحْرِقُهُ كَيْفَ أَمْ ، رَحْمَتِكَ وَ فَضْلِكَ بِأَمَلٍ هُوَ وَ النَّارُ تُؤْلِمُهُ تَعْلَمُ أَنْتَ وَ زَفِيرُهَا عَلَيْهِ يَشْتَمِلُ كَيْفَ أَمْ ، مَكَانَهُ تَرَى وَ صَوْتَهُ تَسْمَعُ كَيْفَ أَمْ ، صِدْقَهُ تَعْلَمُ أَنْتَ وَ أَطْبَاقِهَا بَيْنَ يَتَنَقْلَقُ كَيْفَ أَمْ ، ضَعْفَهُ مِنْهَا عِتْقِهِ فِي فَضْلَكَ يَرْجُو كَيْفَ أَمْ ، رَبَّهُ يَا يُنَادِيكَ هُوَ وَ زَبَانِيَتُهَا تَزْجُرُهُ لَا وَ ، فَضْلِكَ مِنَ الْمَعْرُوفِ لَا وَ ، بِكَ الظَّنَّ ذَلِكَ مَا هَيْهَاتَ ، فِيهَا فَتَتْرُكَهُ أَقْطَعُ فَبِالْيَقِينِ ، إِحْسَانِكَ وَ بِرِّكَ مِنَ الْمُوَحِّدِينَ بِهِ عَامَلْتَ لِمَا مَشِيَّةً إِخْلَادٍ مِنْ بِهِ قَضَيْتَ وَ ، جَاحِدِيكَ تَعْذِيبِ مِنْ بِهِ حَكَمْتَ مَا لَا لَوْ وَ مَقَرًّا فِيهَا لِأَحَدٍ كَانَ مَا وَ ، سَلَاماً وَ بَرْداً كُلَّهَا النَّارَ لَجَعَلْتَ ، مُعَانِدِيكَ الْكَافِرِينَ مِنَ تَمْلَأَهَا أَنْ أَقْسَمْتَ أَسْمَاؤُكَ تَقَدَّسَتْ لَكِنَّكَ ، مُقَاماً لَا جَلَّ أَنْتَ وَ ، الْمُعَانِدِينَ فِيهَا تُخَلِّدَ أَنْ وَ ، أَجْمَعِينَ النَّاسِ وَ الْجِنَّةِ مِنَ كَمَنْ مُؤْمِناً كَانَ أَفَمَنْ ، مُتَكَرِّماً بِالْإِنْعَامِ تَطَوَّلْتَ وَ ، مُبْتَدِئاً قُلْتَ ثَنَاؤُكَ . يَسْتَوُونَ لَا فَاسِقاً كَانَ
الَّتِي بِالْقَضِيَّةِ وَ ، قَدَّرْتَهَا الَّتِي بِالْقُدْرَةِ فَأَسْأَلُكَ سَيِّدِي وَ إِلَهِي هَذِهِ فِي لِي تَهَبَ أَنْ ، أَجْرَيْتَهَا عَلَيْهِ مَنْ غَلَبَتْ وَ ، حَكَمْتَهَا وَ حَتَمْتَهَا كُلَّ وَ ، اذْنَبْتَهُ ذَنْبٍ كُلَّ وَ ، اجْرَمْتُهُ جُرْمِ كُلِّ السَّاعَةِ هَذِهِ فِي وَ اللَّيْلَةِ أَوْ أَخْفَيْتُهُ ، اعْلَنْتُهُ أَوْ كَتَمْتُهُ ، عَمِلْتُهُ جَهْلٍ كُلَّ وَ ، أَسْرَرْتُهُ قَبِيحٍ

وَكَّلْتَهُمُ الَّذِينَ الْكَاتِبِينَ الْكِرَامَ بِإِثْبَاتِهَا أَمَرْتَ سَيِّئَةً كُلَّ وَ ، أَظْهَرْتَهُ كُنْتَ وَ ، جَوَارِحِي مَعَ عَلَيَّ شُهُوداً جَعَلْتَهُمْ وَ ، مِنِّي يَكُونُ مَا يَحْفَظُ بِرَحْمَتِكَ وَ ، عَنْهُمْ خَفِيَ لِمَا الشَّاهِدَ وَ ، وَرَائِهِمْ مِنْ عَلَيَّ الرَّقِيبَ أَنْتَ أَوْ أَنْزَلْتَهُ خَيْرٍ كُلِّ مِنْ حَظِّي تُوَفِّرَ أَنْ وَ ، سَتَرْتَهُ بِفَضْلِكَ وَ ، أَخْفَيْتَهُ أَوْ ، تَغْفِرُهُ ذَنْبٍ أَوْ ، بَسْطَتَهُ رِزْقٍ أَوْ ، نَشَرْتَهُ بِرٍّ أَوْ ، فَضَّلْتَهُ إِحْسَانٍ . رَبِّ يَا رَبِّ يَا رَبِّ يَا ، تَسْتُرُهُ خَطَأٍ

يَا ، نَاصِيَتِي بِيَدِهِ مَنْ يَا ، رِقِّي مَالِكَ وَ مَوْلَايَ وَ سَيِّدِي وَ إِلَهِي يَا يَا رَبِّ يَا رَبِّ ، فَاقَتِي وَ يَفْقُرِي خَبِيراً يَا ، مَسْكَنَتِي وَ يَضُرِّي عَلِيماً تَجْعَلَ أَنْ ، أَسْمَائِكَ وَ صِفَاتِكَ أَعْظَمِ وَ ، قُدْسِكَ وَ بِحَقِّكَ أَسْأَلُكَ ، رَبِّ وَ ، مَوْصُولَةً بِخِدْمَتِكَ وَ ، مَعْمُورَةً بِذِكْرِكَ النَّهَارَ وَ اللَّيْلَ مِنْ أَوْقَاتِي وَاحِداً وِرْداً كُلَّهَا أَوْرَادِي وَ أَعْمَالِي تَكُونَ حَتَّى ، مَقْبُولَةً عِنْدَكَ أَعْمَالِي . سَرْمَداً خِدْمَتِكَ فِي حَالِي وَ ،

يَا رَبِّ يَا ، أَحْوَالِي شَكَوْتُ إِلَيْهِ مَنْ يَا ، مُعَوَّلِي عَلَيْهِ مَنْ يَا سَيِّدِي يَا الْعَزِيمَةَ عَلَى اشْدُدْ وَ ، جَوَارِحِي خِدْمَتِكَ عَلَى قَوِّ ، رَبِّ يَا رَبِّ الِاتِّصَالِ فِي الدَّوَامِ وَ ، خَشْيَتِكَ فِي الْجِدَّ لِي هَبْ وَ ، جَوَانِحِي فِي إِلَيْكَ أَسْرَعَ وَ ، السَّابِقِينَ مَيَادِينَ فِي إِلَيْكَ أَسْرَحَ حَتَّى ، بِخِدْمَتِكَ دُنُوَّ مِنْكَ أَدْنُو وَ ، الْمُشْتَاقِينَ فِي قُرْبِكَ إِلَى اشْتِاقَ وَ ، الْبَارِزِينَ مَعَ جِوَارِكَ فِي اجْتَمِعَ وَ ، الْمُوقِنِينَ مَخَافَةَ أَخَافَكَ وَ ، الْمُخْلِصِينَ . الْمُؤْمِنِينَ

مِنْ اجْعَلْنِي وَ ، فَكِدْهُ كَادَنِي مَنْ وَ ، فَأَرِدْهُ بِسُوءٍ أَرَادَنِي مَنْ وَ اللَّهُمَّ زُلْفَةً أَخَصِّهِمْ وَ ، مِنْكَ مَنْزِلَةً أَقْرَبِهِمْ وَ ، عِنْدَكَ نَصِيباً عَبِيدِكَ أَحْسَنْ عَلَيَّ اعْطِفْ وَ ، يَجُودُكَ لِي جُدْ وَ ، يَفْضِلِكَ إِلَّا ذَلِكَ يُنَالُ لَا فَإِنَّهُ ، لَدَيْكَ قَلْبِي وَ ، لَهِجاً بِذِكْرِكَ لِسَانِي اجْعَلْ وَ ، بِرَحْمَتِكَ احْفَظْنِي وَ ، بِمَجْدِكَ اغْفِرْ وَ ، عَثْرَتِي أَقِلْنِي وَ ، إِجَابَتِكَ يُحْسِنْ عَلَيَّ مَنْ وَ ، مُتَيَّماً يُحِبُّكَ وَ ، بِدُعَائِكَ آمَرْتَهُمْ وَ ، يِعِبَادَتِكَ عِبَادَكَ عَلَى قَضَيْتَ فَإِنَّكَ ، زَلَّتِي مَدَدْتُ رَبِّ يَا إِلَيْكَ وَ ، وَجْهِي نَصَبْتُ رَبِّ يَا قَالَيْكَ ، الْإِجَابَةَ لَهُمْ ضَمِنْتَ مِنْ تَقْطَعْ لَا وَ ، مُنَايَ بَلِّغْنِي وَ ، دُعَائِي لِي اسْتَجِبْ فَيُعِزَّتِكَ ، يَدِي . أَعْدَائِي مِنْ الْإِنْسِ وَ الْجِنِّ شَرَّ اكْفِنِي وَ ، رَجَائِي فَضْلِكَ

يَا ، تَشَاءُ لِمَا فَعَّالٌ فَإِنَّكَ ، الدُّعَاءَ إِلَّا يَمْلِكُ لَا لِمَنْ اغْفِرْ الرِّضَا سَرِيعَ يَا مَالِهِ رَأْسٍ مِنْ ارْحَمْ ، غِنًى طَاعَتُهُ وَ شِفَاءٌ ذِكْرُهُ وَ دَوَاءٌ اسْمُهُ مِنْ نُورٌ يَا ، النِّقَمِ دَافِعَ يَا ، النِّعَمِ سَابِغَ يَا ، الْبُكَاءَ سِلَاحُهُ وَ ، الرَّجَاءَ آلِ وَ مُحَمَّدٍ عَلَى صَلِّ ، يَعْلَمُ لَا عَالِماً يَا ، الظُّلْمَ فِي الْمُسْتَوْحِشِينَ الْأَئِمَّةَ وَ رَسُولَهُ عَلَى اللَّهُ صَلَّى وَ ، أَهْلُهُ أَنْتَ مَا بِي افْعَلْ وَ ، مُحَمَّدٍ كَثِيراً تَسْلِيماً سَلَّمَ وَ ، آلِهِ مِنْ الْمَيَامِينَ

www.ingramcontent.com/pod-product-compliance
Lightning Source LLC
Chambersburg PA
CBHW051555010526
44118CB00022B/2721